Moments
with *Miley*

Tara and Miley Share
with You Life Lessons
To Inspire and Enrich
Your Life.

TARA BORGHESE

MOTIVATE AND INSPIRE OTHERS!

"Share This Book"

Retail $24.95

Special Quantity Discounts

5-20 Books	$21.95
21-99 Books	$18.95
100-499 Books	$15.95
500-999 Books	$10.95
1,000+ Books	$8.95

To Place an Order Contact:

Email: support@momentswithmiley.com

Website: momentswithmiley.com

Instagram: moments_with_miley

FaceBook: Moments with Miley

THE IDEAL PROFESSIONAL SPEAKER FOR YOUR NEXT EVENT!

Any organization that wants to develop their people to become "extraordinary," needs to hire Tara for a keynote and/or workshop training!

To Contact or Book Tara to Speak:
Email: support@momentswithmiley.com
Website: momentswithmiley.com
Instagram: moments_with_miley
FaceBook: Moments with Miley

DEDICATION

I'd like to say thank you to

Christopher Borghese,
Who continually encourages me to
keep growing on this journey.

Miley,
Thank you for your unconditional
love and being my inspiration.

Drew, Amanda, and Brady,
Thank you for allowing me to grow
as a person while being your mom.

TABLE OF CONTENTS

INTRODUCTION

WITH NUMEROUS OPPORTUNITIES in front of each of us to invest our time and money; investing in our own personal development will yield a far greater return than any other venture.

About 7 years ago I set out on a path of becoming more self aware of my actions and my motives behind them. I knew that my current skill set was not going to get me where I wanted to go. So I began to gather books and audios from some of the most respected leaders of personal development, leaders such as Jim Rohn, Dale Carnegie, Brian Tracy, Jack Canfield and my own personal mentor James Malinchak. I quickly realized how my own lack of personal growth had impacted every job, relationship, and project that I had ever been apart of. I used to think I was a positive person until I started hanging around positive people. I had some growing to do and I was ready to take action! I couldn't get enough; I was hooked on discovering my full potential.

As I began to implement some of the strategies I was learning, my life started to head in a more positive direction, one with purpose and clarity. One evening while reflecting on the day's events, my sweet little 15-pound Shih Tzu Miley snuggled up at my feet. As I looked down at her it was as if a spotlight turned on to illuminate her character. So much of what I was learning Miley was already living in her daily life.

While I worked on increasing my people skills, Miley won friends instantly and effortlessly. As I took inventory of my life trying to get focused on my goals, Miley knew exactly what she wanted and how to get it. While I tried to fit rest into each day, Miley has the perfect balance between rest and play. Watching how Miley enjoys each moment of her day models what it means to "enjoy the journey." I would never have imagined that one of my greatest teachers of human personal development would be my dog!

Allow me to introduce to you the next great teacher of personal development: the talented, the inspiring, the furry: ***Miss Miley!***

Cheers From The Crowd

Miley's story began in the spring of 2009 when our youngest son Brady informed us that he wanted a Shih Tzu puppy. We headed to our trusted local breeder to pick out our new family member. The moment we laid eyes on Miley playing with her 5 littermates, we knew our family would never be the same.

Miley's unique personality showed itself right away. Whenever there is a loud noise, Miley will do the moonwalk back into corners: totally adorable! While attempting to bark, she throws her head back and moves her mouth but barely makes a sound. Eventually, she musters up a small bark that gets her point across. My husband often teases that Miley is like the penguin from the film *Toy Story* who swallowed his squeaker. We are convinced this is why Miley's mission in life is to rip open toys and steal their squeakers!

Miley is the sweetest dog; she never growls, nips, or acts temperamental towards humans or other dogs. She has such a sweet disposition and funny personality. She is truly a gift to be treasured.

I thought it a bit selfish not to share with the world the life changing and fun moments that we have experienced together. Watching Miley has taught me so much about my own personal development, and I am honored and privileged to share this wealth of wisdom with you. I just know that throughout this book she will steal your heart while teaching you how to become successful in your own personal development.

Moment #1...

PEOPLE SKILLS

MILEY HAS MAD people skills! It's been said that dogs are the greatest winners of friends. No matter who comes to the door: the pizza delivery person, a package carrier, or a neighbor, Miley leaves them feeling as if they were *expected* and *anticipated*. You may be thinking, "How can a dog have good people skills?" Did you know that 93% of all communication is non-verbal? This is how Miley can say to each person we pass on our daily walks "hello" and "have a great day!"

Since the first day we brought Miley into our home and lives, she has greeted every person she's met with love and enthusiasm. Miley shows her excitement by wagging her tail and sniffing the person from head to toe. She is genuinely interested in finding out everything there is to know about the person by putting on her Sherlock Holms detective cap and getting to work. She can sniff out where they've been, what they ate for lunch and whom they've hung out with. Her ability to be more interested in the person in front of her than herself almost always results in both parties getting what they each want. Miley gets what she desires: a kind word, a soft belly rubbing, or a scratching behind her ears and the person walks away feeling loved. It has been proven through science that when we pet a dog it triggers the release of the hormone <u>oxytocin</u>, widely referred to as the love hormone or the cuddle chemical. It can also lower your heart rate and reduce blood pressure. That seems like a pretty good deal on our part as humans. (1)

You see… we all need people in our lives for the whole give and take concept to work. Miley gets that if she has a good time meeting new people, they will have a good time meeting her.

Dogs remind us that we need to engage in people's lives to have meaningful interactions. Unlike Miley, most of us are more interested in ourselves; we are our **own** favorite topic.

One of the best selling books of all time is *How To Win Friends And Influence People* by Dale Carnegie. I highly recommend this book if your people skills are not as good as your dogs. Mr. Carnegie tells a story in this book about a lesson that his dog Tippy taught him as a boy:

> *"You never read a book on psychology, Tippy. You didn't need to. You knew by some divine instinct that you could make more friends in two months by becoming genuinely interested in other people than you could in two years by trying to get other people interested in you"* (2)

No matter what business or walk of life you are in, it is second to the *business of people.*

We can all get so busy that we don't even see what the people around us are going through. We don't know the kind of day the lady in the drive-thru is having or what the gentleman cleaning the windows at the office is struggling with. A simple smile with a "Hello! How's your day going" can actually brighten someone's day.

What about the people we are closest to? Our family and friends tend to be the people we get "used" to without even realizing it. No matter if I leave the house for 5 minutes or 5 hours Miley greets me the same way…with animation and enthusiasm. Let us all learn from Miley and greet people the way she does, with genuine interest and love.

TRAINING TIPS

- 🐾 Greet people with a genuine excitement.

- 🐾 Smile and say hello to people during your day.

- 🐾 Become more aware of your
  non-verbal communication

- 🐾 Find out what interests the person you're talking to.

*"Always leave everyone you meet
wagging their tail!"
—Miley*

I ♥ My Shih Tzu

Moment #2...

ENJOY THE JOURNEY

MILEY'S FAVORITE PART of each day is her neighborhood walk. From the moment the front door opens she greets the world with optimism, expecting that this walk will be the best walk ever! We are blessed to live in southern California where the weather is nice just about everyday, which makes walking Miley very enjoyable. However, there are times when we are busy or tired, and we want to hurry it up a bit. At these moments our objective is to have her just get her business done so we can move on with our day. But no-no-no...Miley will not be hurried. It's all about the journey for her, smelling the bushes, stopping to admire the bicyclist, and watching the neighbor's cat scale the fence. Let us not forget, Miley can't do her deed just anywhere; she energetically seeks out the perfect spot where the magic will happen, much like a photographer searches out the perfect angle of light. She is not focused on getting from point A to point B; it's truly all about the journey.

When Miley turns that last corner and can see that our house is not far off she slows down to look around in all directions. There are times when she comes to a complete stop and sits down. This action is not her stubbornness coming out; it is meditative. She uses all her senses to experience and savor the moment. She puts her nose up to sniff, feels the wind blowing on her face, and intently looks around at her surroundings.

It's as if Miley knows these walks are special, she doesn't want to get in such a hurry that she misses something meaningful.

Watching Miley has inspired me to start practicing living in the moment in my own life. Whether I am at a coffee shop or at lunch with my husband, I will gaze around to observe all the different conversations that are taking place around us…sometimes we like to guess if that couple sitting 2 tables over from us is married, friends, or perhaps on their first date. Another way I am practicing this valuable lesson is becoming more mindful at daily activities. Multi-tasking had become my best friend and I knew the time had come to say "good-bye" to her. I am learning to focus on one thing at a time until it's complete; this habit is a little harder to break. I am in training to experience the world around me with all my senses fully engaged like Miley has taught me.

Most of us are busier than ever in this fast paced technology driven world. With work, social media, countless distractions, and e-mail overload it's hard to remember to just take a moment. The next time you smell the aroma of fresh baked bread, see a beautiful colored flower, or feel the warm water of your shower run over body… stop and remember that this moment was meant for you to enjoy.

TRAINING TIPS

- 🐾 Slow down, don't be in such a hurry
- 🐾 Connect with your thoughts and feelings
- 🐾 Look around to see if you're missing anything important, be aware of your surroundings.
- 🐾 Practice living in the present instead of trying to multi-task.

"Stop and smell the roses,
or you may never know
who peed on them"
— Miley

Moment #3...

LISTENING SKILLS

I HAVE TO say that Miley is the best listener, and not just because she rarely interrupts me or thinks everything I have to say is interesting and worth listening to.

When I ask her questions, she tilts her cute little head to the side, and I believe she is intently trying to understand what I am saying. Miley actively participates in the conversation by keeping eye contact and turning her head from side to side. She never checks her messages on her very popular Instagram account during our talks, which I appreciate.

Miley has discovered the difference between "hearing" and "listening." For example, Miley will be completely asleep in one of her cozy little beds when all of a sudden she sits straight up at full attention. Her ears go upright and she moves them in the direction she heard the sound coming from. She waits and listens to see if she should jump out of bed and start barking or lie back down and continue her nap.

Miley's response demonstrates that there is a clear difference between "hearing" and "listening." She "heard" a sound, but she had to "listen" to determine how to respond or react.

Studies have proven a dog is capable of hearing frequencies 2 times that of the average human. Did you also know that a dog has more than 18 muscles that enable them to move their ears in the direction of a sound? Truly amazing is a dog's ability to hear their world around them.

If we're not careful, we can get caught in a trap of hearing the people around us, but not really listening to what they are saying. When it comes to communication, listening is a far more valuable skill than speaking. We all learned to speak by listening first, yet listening seems to be the least practiced.

If you have ever needed to express your feelings, good or bad, then you know the value of having a good listener in your life. When someone simply listens without trying to work everything out, it makes the other person feel respected and valued. This could possibly be why there is such a strong bond between man and dog.

The tone in which the person talking might actually be more important than their words. Once, I walked into the living room where Miley had decorated it with toilet paper; I thought this was only something my teenagers did. She carefully listened for my tone to determine if she was in trouble or not. If my voice is deep and scolding she will creep away and sulk a bit, however if I speak to her excitedly, her tail will wag and she'll think, "Hey, she likes what I've done with the place." Tone is very important in Miley's listening skills toolbox.

Over the years, I have had to employ my best listening skills to determine what the heck Miley is saying. I fully expect words to come out of her mouth any day now, but until then, I have to listen intently to understand the meaning behind each bark and whine.

Miley has many different barks. (Granted not much noise comes out)

Here are a few of her most popular:
1. I'm hungry fill my bowl bark
2. I'm going to pee my pants bark
3. Someone's at the door; it's the pizza I ordered bark
4. I heard something and our security has been breached bark

Miley and I are together just about every day; so it is just as important for me to understand her language as well as she understands mine.

TRAINING TIPS

- 🐾 Look people in the eye when they are talking
- 🐾 Give people your full attention; don't be distracted
- 🐾 Be aware of your non-verbal communication
- 🐾 Actively participate in your daily conversations by listening not just hearing (Don't forget tone)

"Recipe for great communication is: two parts listening, one part barking"

—Miley

Moment #4...
POWER OF FOCUS

THIS IS ONE of the most powerful moments that I've witnessed from Miley. Since Miley is an only "child" she gets all the attention and all the toys! I absolutely love to shop… particularly for toys that I think Miley will enjoy. There is not a store with a dog section that I haven't combed through in search of the next great toy for her.

If Miley were to make a mission statement for her life, removing all the stuffing and squeakers from her toys would top the list. She has a top-secret system in place to achieve this goal that she hasn't shared with us civilians. Any given day could be the day that Miley prances over to one of her toy baskets and choses the "one." Some toys have been around for months while others only weeks. Once the special toy that will gain her focused attention is chosen, let the fun begin!

What makes this process so interesting is that Miley only does this 6-8 times per year. She becomes so focused on her goal of removing that squeaker that she becomes unstoppable. Her normal routine of eating, walking, and drinking becomes a distraction during this event. I have witnessed her turn an entire toy inside out through a hole no bigger than a dime... now that's serious skills. This effort and determination usually lasts anywhere from 4-36 hours depending on how well made the stuffed toy is. This focused effort always ends with Miley getting the coveted squeaker and running through the house with it for all to see; this has become known as her victory lap.

Her focus, determination and clarity of her mission are truly inspiring. I am convinced that Miley's success is due to her unusual ability to get clear about what she wants. Once the commitment is made she becomes enthusiastic about the goal ahead of her and there is no turning back.

Focus means to concentrate on one center of interest. This is best demonstrated when planning a wedding. Deadlines are set, dresses are ordered, invitations are sent and the list goes on. So much focused thought and planning goes into making this one-day event a day to remember. Imagine what your life would look like if you put that much focused attention into designing it.

Most of us are so busy with life's commitments that our goals have gotten out of focus and fuzzy. Now is the time to adjust that lens and bring clarity to what is working in our lives and let go of the things that aren't. It's been said that whatever we focus on grows. That can be a comforting thought or a very scary one. Change your focus if need be, because whatever you choose to focus on will become your reality.

TRAINING TIPS

- 🐾 Get Clear! What area in your life do you want to make a positive change in? (Health, finances, relationship, etc....)
- 🐾 Get Excited! Excitement can spark momentum.
- 🐾 Take Action! Stop procrastinating
- 🐾 Don't Quit! Don't stop until you get that squeaker!

"If you chase two squirrels, you won't catch any."

— Miley

(Warning: do not let your dog chew and swallow the plastic squeaker)

Moment #5...

STRETCHING

ISN'T IT AMAZING that dogs instinctively know to stretch before exercise? We humans however need to be reminded of its importance and benefits from time to time. One of the first things Miley does in the morning upon waking is to stretch her body. She also stretches before every walk she takes. One of her favorite things to do is to roll over on her back and do a full body stretch. I perform a similar move in Pilates where I pretend to touch one wall with my toes and the other with my fingertips. This move elongates the muscles and improves flexibility. As Miley gets older it will be more important than ever for her to remain flexible to prevent injury and the same goes for us.

As I reflect on the many physical benefits of stretching daily for staying flexible, I am reminded of the first time

I heard that professional football players were learning ballet. The players that were flexible in their thinking and willing to be "stretched" saw the value that learning ballet could have for their overall performance. You see, these players knew that to achieve the highest performance in their sport, they would have to be willing to be stretched in more ways than one. They would have to be open to a new idea, a new way of doing things.

I can't ignore this same principle in the area of personal development. If we remain stagnant or too comfortable in any area of our lives, we will become inflexible.

Sometimes being stretched is painful and challenging; our thinking can become ridged just like our muscles. Our comfort zone has become the "familiar" is most of our lives; we know it well and it provides a feeling of safety. Going outside that zone is the unknown, the unfamiliar. Let's face it; that can seem a bit scary. We can choose to open ourselves up to new ideas or instead limit our thoughts to past experiences. Stretching will make room for us to hold more of the good stuff.

Learning new information that stretches our minds will create endless possibilities in every area of our lives. Don't limit your growth by doing the same ole, same ole. Pursue new ideas, read a book, learn a new board game, a new social media platform, or finally pursue that business idea you've been putting off.

The next time you are stretching your muscles don't forget that your mind could use some exercise as well.

TRAINING TIPS

- 🐾 Become better at problem solving through playing games
- 🐾 Increase your creativity by learning a craft or new hobby
- 🐾 Learning a new skill at home or work
- 🐾 Get outside your comfort zone and try something new

"Paws a moment to stretch your body and your mind"

—Miley

Moment #6...
COMPASSION

*Compassion: sympathetic pity and concern for
the sufferings or misfortunes of others.*

AS YOU MAY already know, animals of all kinds have been
known to show amazing compassion. There are numerous
videos on YouTube that show how animals from an elephant
to a black lab have saved the life of another animal. These
stories are not only heart warming but also inspiring.

Miley had an older sister named Holly (also a Shih-Tzu).
When Miley joined our family in June of 2009, she was the
new kid on the block, so to speak, so she had to quickly learn
her place in the "pack." Holly accepted Miley at a distance
and really wasn't all that interested in her. Miley, being
the playful pup, tried to coax Holly into some wrestling

matches and at times Holly would indulge her if she felt like it. Holly's favorite past time was sitting at my feet and sleeping, so Miley was really just a fuzzy annoyance as far as Holly was concerned. Most of their interactions took place at the front door whenever the doorbell rang. Since Miley was younger and faster she almost always beat Holly to the door, pushing her back with her boxing skills (Miley uses her paws to play fight). What true sisters they were!

Holly struggled with some health issues, and they started to get worse the beginning of 2011. Holly suffered from a collapsed trachea and an enlarged heart, so when she caught what is known as "kennel cough" it was devastating to her health. My husband and I would take turns holding her upright on our chests each night so that Holly could get some rest. For six weeks straight we did this until she got over it, it was like having a newborn baby all over again.

After that prolonged illness, Holly started having seizures and her health continued to decline. Remarkably, Miley picked up on the fact that Holly was sick. At times she would just lay next to her to keep her company. Miley took on a new role as protector and caregiver to her sister. She knew not to play fight with Holly anymore, instead she would check up on her, as if to say, "If you need anything I'm here." Miley demonstrated true concern and compassion until the very end. Holly passed away March of 2011.

If anyone in the family is hurt, sick, or just feeling sad, Miley will come to their aid. She is truly an amazing example to us all. I am convinced that if Miley were human she would have chosen to become a nurse.

You don't have to be a nurse, missionary, or Miley to be able to show compassion to others. Take a look around, there are a lot of hurting people in this world.

The good news is we have all been given the ability to show compassion to those hurting or suffering around us. The desire to show compassion crosses all boundaries of race, religion, and even species. This is the Golden Rule…"*Treat others the way you want to be treated.*" I believe that Miley lives by this each and everyday.

TRAINING TIPS

- Practice being attuned to others needs, you could be the answer to their prayer

- One way to show compassion to someone is to say kind words; everyone loves to be genuinely complimented.

- Kindness is contagious…go "infect" some people.

- Carry out random and intentional acts of kindness without expecting anything in return.

"If you want your face licked, then lick someone else's"

—Miley

Moment #7...

FORGIVENESS

FORGIVENESS IS A fundamental key to a happy life, and Miley knows it! Since Miley is a small dog she has this incredible ability to get under peoples feet. Since we live with her, we all know to be aware of where she is, but occasionally a guest will unknowingly step on her tail or on one of her paws (sad I know). Miley will yelp, move away from the accident, and allow the person to apologize. She then sits next to the person while they pet her and tell her how sorry they are. In response, she licks their hand and gives them her, "I accept your apology and I forgive you" look. Miley doesn't run away and analyze if they really meant it or decide if she should hold a grudge; she immediately forgives and moves on.

Miley gets to practice forgiveness everyday when I leave the house without her. She is a lap dog and that is exactly where she wants to be most of the time. I can hardly resist the power of her big brown eyes looking at me as if to say, "Can I come? Pretty please?" She will lie down in front of the door so if there's any chance of her coming, we won't be able to forget her. We literally have to step over her to leave the house (so stinking cute!) I feel so bad that I will start telling her how sorry I am that she can't come with me. If you are a dog owner, which I suspect you are, then I am sure you've experienced this a time or two. She seems so sad and disappointed when we leave, but so full of love and excitement when we return! Again, she holds no grudges. She is free to love and enjoy our time together upon my return.

This topic of forgiveness can trigger different reactions in each of us depending on our mindset. I used to believe that holding onto a grudge against someone that had hurt me would somehow hurt him or her. Boy was I wrong! The only person that was still being hurt was myself. Forgiveness is a funny thing; we need to offer it even when the person that hurt us does not ask for it. Forgiveness never excuses the behavior; it prevents it from destroying you. Forgiveness allows us to move forward with our lives.

One more quick moment with Miley about forgiveness:

(Miley has given me permission to share this story)

When Miley was a puppy, she did some naughty things that she wouldn't be proud of today. As a puppy she liked to chew on our baseboards and shred the newspaper we would put down for her. She would wait until she knew she was alone to commit these crimes. When we would catch her in the act of vandalism, she would put her little tail between her legs and walk slowly into her crate. We could clearly see that she felt bad about what she had done. After the mess was cleaned up, we would let her know she could come out and join the family.

She would stand up, wag her tail, and come sprinting out with joy!

What Miley demonstrated is self-forgiveness. We forgave her and we all moved on in our relationship. Most of the time it is easier to forgive others than our own self. We are the hardest on ourselves when it comes to our own wrongs. We will all make mistakes in our lifetime but how we choose to deal with them will determine the level of peace we can experience.

Forgiveness is the best gift you can give yourself!

TRAINING TIPS

- 🐾 Let go of grudges!
- 🐾 Forgive quickly those that have wronged you.
- 🐾 Receive and give apologies when necessary
- 🐾 Love yourself by forgiving yourself!

"When someone extends the hand of forgiveness, don't bite it"

—Miley

Moment #8...

LIFE'S STORMS

WE WILL ALL go through a storm or two in our lives; how we handle them can make all the difference. This is the moment with Miley that inspired the creation of this book.

The picture on the opposite page was captured right after a terrible thunderstorm that sent Miley running for cover. Even when Miley was a puppy, she disliked loud noises. When startled, she would seek shelter in the corner of her puppy crate. What didn't make this any better was our move to North Carolina. What an absolutely beautiful state. With thunderstorms that make you believe you have a front row seat to a fireworks extravaganza. Needless to say Miley, was not a fan.

It was a warm Saturday afternoon in June when the gentle rumble of thunder started to roll in. Miley was sitting on my lap while I read a book on the family room sofa. Her ears perked up and she looked at me to see if I also heard it. I reassured her by petting her and telling her she was safe; this seemed to work until the next big boom. This pattern repeated for about 10 minutes until the storm got closer and louder. One large explosion right over the house sent Miley running for cover! She jumped off the couch and headed to her favorite "bomb shelter:" under our bed.

No amount of coaxing was going to get her to change her mind. She had a plan, and she was sticking to it.

Miley stayed hidden under the bed until the storm finally passed. When I knelt down on the floor to check on her and to inform her that it was safe to come out, she hesitantly came half way out and stopped. She took a look around, put her ears up to listen if the storm had passed and slowly emerged from under the bed. Confident that the storm had indeed blown by, Miley began to run and play as usual. Life was good again!

I returned to the sofa to ponder what had just happened. I thought about some of the questions that may have been going through her head like, "*how long is this going to last?*" and "*will I make it out of here safely?*" Observing how Miley knew exactly where to go to feel safe and protected during a storm was very impressive. This was her designated safety zone. When caught outside during a thunderstorm you will see people running for cover just like Miley did; it's instinctual. But lets turn this to a different kind of storm, you know the ones in life that catch us off guard…an illness, a layoff, or the sudden death of a loved one.

The saying goes like this: life is 10% what happens to you and 90% how you respond. We can't always control what life sends our way, but we can control how we react! Miley didn't become a victim or spend the rest of the day complaining about the storm, she found a solution, took cover, and when it was safe to come out…she did! The good news about storms is that they **will** pass and the sun **will** come out again.

If you are still hiding "under the bed" now is the time to come out, open up the windows and enjoy life.

Storms are a part of life, without them nothing would grow. Without the rain we wouldn't have flowers and without extreme heat gold couldn't be refined.

Sure, another storm may pop up unexpectedly, but remember that you get to choose how much damage it does.

TRAINING TIPS

🐾 Take cover if you need to, but remember it's only temporary.

🐾 Have faith that the sun will come out again.

🐾 Remember that you have control over how you respond.

🐾 Growth occurs after a storm.

"When the storms of life come your way, adjust your tails."
—Miley

Moment #9...

DON'T LOOK BACK

EVERY SO OFTEN Miley has been known to get distracted on her walks. Usually she stays on the path and enjoys the next upcoming bush or neighbor ahead, but on occasion, she becomes fixated on what's going on behind her. This can be challenging to the family member that's walking her because having to remind her to focus on the path ahead can be very repetitive. One of Miley's nicknames is "Mrs. Kravitz: the neighborhood busy body." Every neighborhood has one and Miley is ours. She's earned this title honestly. There have been times on our walks where Miley is so distracted that she actually forgets to do her business. The silver lining in this for our neighbors is that Miley doesn't speak English and can't tell all their secrets.

While being her nosey self, she tends to look behind her instead of the path ahead. The disadvantage to Miley choosing to look behind her rather than in front is that she puts herself at risk of loosing her footing. A few weeks ago on our walk, she became so interested in the German Shepard that was on his morning walk behind us that she slipped trying to step up on the curb and hit her chin on the concrete. She immediately shook it off with a bit of embarrassment and ran into the house. I think her ego (if dogs have egos) was bruised more than her chin. Looking back caused Miley to lose sight of the path ahead of her.

This example holds so much truth for our lives that I had to include it.

Looking back can represent living in the past for some of us. There is a very popular quote from an unknown author that states, "You can't start the next chapter of your life if you keep re-reading the last one."

Maybe you started a business that failed, perhaps you tried to lose weight and didn't, or you had a bad relationship break-up. These events are all apart of life and learning. Your past does not have to define your future.

My dad taught me a valuable life lesson while teaching me to drive. While I was adjusting the mirrors in preparation for my lesson he said, "Keep your eyes on the road ahead. Only glance in the rearview mirror. It can only tell you where you've been, not where you're going."

Don't let the failures or hurts of your past distract you from the blessings in front of you today. Learn from your past, have big dreams for your future, and live in the moment.

TRAINING TIPS

- 🐾 Learn from your past, don't dwell there
- 🐾 Be alert in the now to receive todays blessings
- 🐾 Your past does not define your future
- 🐾 Keep your eyes forward so you don't trip and fall

"When your past barks,
don't answer. It has
nothing new to say"
—Miley

Moment #10...
REMAIN PLAYFUL

IF THERE'S ONE thing that Miley excels at, it's playing. She absolutely loves her collection of stuffed turtles and ducks. She has two toy baskets that are filled to overflowing. I mentioned in an earlier chapter that I find it hard to resist checking out every doggie toy department that I pass. Miley and shopping: my two favorite things in life coming together like a beautiful partnership.

Miley has a childlike spirit about her that her older sister Holly did not possess. Holly had an "old and wise" soul, whereas Miley is more like a toddler; she puts everything in her mouth and leaves it covered in slobber. If any of us approach her toy basket Miley jumps to her feet to investigate what we are doing. She has appointed herself "Guardian of all Toys." I find it fascinating how Miley's personality is so different than Holly's was. Miley will play fetch and give her stuffed duck the death shake all day long where Holly's response to a toy thrown down the hallway was, "You threw it, you go get it."

Miley's playfulness comes out in other ways as well, like her relentless curiosity to explore new things. When a package is delivered to the house Miley gets so excited that she could almost unwrap it with her incessant sniffing. The contents of the package is not what is causing her delight; it's the arrival of possibilities. Whether it's the new hot pink wedges that I had to have or the latest video game for my son, Miley exhibits a spirit of endless wonder and excitement. It's like a surprise birthday party every time the doorbell rings.

Remaining playful and childlike is one of the secrets to enjoying life to its fullest. If you are an adult reading this book, let Miley inspire you to do something fun. Sing karaoke with some friends, watch a funny dog (or cat) video on YouTube, or build a tent in your living room with the sofa cushions. Give yourself permission to laugh out loud and act silly. Keeping a youthful spirit about yourself will not only make you more fun to be around, but it's a valuable tool for diffusing stress. George Bernard Shaw a

Nobel Prize writer and Oscar-winning Irish playwright once said, *"We don't stop playing because we grow old; we grow old because we stop playing."* In the busy responsible world of being a grown-up remember the freedom of childlike playfulness.

TRAINING TIPS

- ❖ Chase after the ice cream truck next time it's in your neighborhood
- ❖ Rent a funny movie and laugh
- ❖ Play catch with your favorite canine
- ❖ Remember what it felt like to pretend and dream

"Dogs are just grown up puppies, after all"
— Miley

Moment #11...

THE POWER OF TOUCH

THE ONLY THING Miley loves more than having me pet her; is bacon. Since it's not good for her to eat bacon all day, I have opted to show her my love through scratching her ears, rubbing her belly and massaging her legs frequently throughout the day.

Whenever I am watching a movie or reading on the couch, Miley is right in the middle of the action, propped up next to me making sure that she is as close to me as she can get. Often times she will climb right up into my lap, earning the term "lap dog." She loves to feel close and safe with me through touch; this non-verbal way that we connect with each other is invaluable for us both.

More and more research is showing that animals experience multiple benefits through touch. I have raised three human children and two canine and have witnessed how powerful touch can be to both. Just like humans, canines experience increased circulation, greater flexibility, and bonding through physical touch. Touch is said to be as basic of a need as food and water to our canine's overall wellbeing. Massaging and petting our furry babies can calm anxiety, relieve pain, and ease loneliness.

A recent study at Arizona State University revealed that dogs preferred being petted to receiving verbal praise. (3) The study also found that dogs showed no interest in the people that just talked to them. What? I thought that Miley hung on every word I spoke! So now I just praise her while I pet her, problem solved! This study does not negate the fact that dogs are able to learn verbal commands with positive rewards; it was done to show the importance of touch.

In the chapter on "People Skills," I talked about the benefits we humans receive from petting a dog, but did you know that the dog actually shares in these same benefits of lowered heart rate and blood pressure? The effects of touch are as powerful to humans as it is to our furry companions. Maybe our dogs are more like us than we thought.

We humans convey many emotions through touch: we comfort someone grieving with a soft hug, congratulate a team member with a high-five, and extend our hand to welcome a stranger. Touch is vital to our ability to bond with each other and live a healthier more affectionate life. Outside of schools and office environments, there is a revolution to restore the power of touch to our society. There are volunteers in hospitals where their only job is to hug and or massage the patient' shoulders. This holds true for humans entering this world as well as leaving it. If you or your canine is touch deprived do something about it today and give each other a hug!

TRAINING TIPS

- 🐾 Give at least 8-12 hugs a day
- 🐾 Learn how to give your dog a massage
- 🐾 Get a massage for yourself, your body will thank you
- 🐾 Incorporate healthy touch into your daily healthy habits

"You can never get too many hugs, or too much bacon"

—Miley

Moment #12...
REST

MILEY HAS MASTERED rest, some days a bit too well. This is never more evident than when we have company stop by, namely the grandkids. Miley absolutely loves playing with our 4 year old grandson, Noah. He immediately races over to her basket and starts pulling out each toy one by one. At first Miley thought this was about as much fun as an IRS audit, but over time she has accepted the game as a sort of search and rescue expedition. She runs from toy to toy sniffing making sure they're all accounted for. Before long, Miley has run a 5k, and she hasn't left the living room. Noah moves on to his second favorite activity: playing cards. Since Miley always loses at Go Fish, she finds this the opportune time to sneak away into the quiet office where she can rest and recharge.

Miley is very aware of her body's need for down time and I admire this about her. She plays very vigorously, but she rests with that same determination. She doesn't just plop down in the middle of the party and expect to get any rest; no, she retreats to a place where she knows she'll be undisturbed. She will step into her comfy bed with the 2" memory foam, turn around a couple of times to ensure the perfect spot and sink into a deep slumber.

About 30-60 minutes later, Miley will emerge like a recharged battery ready to resume play exactly where she left off. She instinctively knows that for her to be fully engaged, she must have balance between rest and play. For Miley, rest is purely physical, but for us humans, it's so much more.

In many religious beliefs, rest is a fundamental requirement for maintaining a healthy body, mind, and soul. We were created to rest regularly. In our results driven society, this concept of rest can elude us. I know the struggle of trying to find the time to rest when there is a never-ending to do list. We can carry this busyness into our so-called vacations as well. Have you ever needed a vacation from your vacation?

I have heard it said, "I'll rest when I'm dead." This may make for a great motivational video, but the truth in research has found that lack of rest increases stress levels, which can lead to chronic health problems over time. Regular lack of sleep puts you at risk of obesity and heart disease, as well as shortens your life expectancy.

Allow me to address a different form of rest: meditation or quite time. Meditation is a time set aside for reflection and relaxation. This gives us time to gain clarity about issues we are facing. It allows us to operate with clear judgment and optimism. This is a time to reflect on the good things in our lives and practice an attitude of gratitude. We are whole beings that require proper maintenance and care. After all, if God was able to take a day off than that's good enough for me.

TRAINING TIPS

- 🐾 Make rest a priority in your life
- 🐾 Plan your rest…add it to your calendar!
- 🐾 Take a walk in the park and take 10 deep breaths
- 🐾 Fully engage in your rest time. Make your to-do list and set it aside

"Life is a balance between REST and finding squeakers"
—Miley

FINAL WORDS

I TRUST YOU have enjoyed this book as well as getting to know Miley through the lens of personal development.

It has been an honor to share my stories of how Miley has inspired me to train and grow in my personal life.

As you can see, Miley has been one of my most influential and best teachers. Her life has been a living example for me to learn from. These twelve moments are just a few of the teachable principles that have propelled me forward to lead a more inspiring and positive life.

Unfortunately, when it comes to personal development there are no "hacks" and you can't outsource it to someone else. To see lasting change in your life takes commitment and a desire to succeed. I am confident that if you apply the principles in this book that have transformed my life and countless others, your life will be richer.

My hope is that you will implement the training tips throughout this book to form new habits that will result in better relationships in your personal and professional life. Personal development is not a one-time investment; it's an account you can deposit into each day and reap the rewards for a lifetime. It's never too late to become the best "*you*" you can be.

Miley and I will continue this journey called life as long as time permits. We will listen, hug, and forgive quickly. We will continue to take long car rides enjoying the scenery and greet the people we meet along the way with excitement and enthusiasm. We will show compassion when needed and tell a joke when appropriate. We will weather life's storms together and bask in the warmth of the sun. We will keep the important things in focus and allow the rest to blur themselves out. We will keep our eyes forward and not allow the past to trip us up. We will continue to put ourselves on the schedule every day for stretching and restful meditation. Last but not least, we will chase after the neighborhood ice cream truck in hopes of finding bacon-flavored ice cream.

"Put your best paw forward."
—*Miley*

CITATIONS

1. Becker, Mikkel *"How Petting a Dog Benefits the Pooch and you."* Vetstreet.com, Published 5 Nov. 2014, Accessed 15 March 2016

2. Carnegie, Dale. *"How to Win Friends and Influence People."* New York: Simon & Schuster, Inc., 1936, Print.

3. Howard, Jacqueline *"Dogs Prefer Petting Way More Than you Thought"*. Huffington Post.com, Published 7 September 2014, Accessed 15 March 2016.

WAIT!!! THERE'S MORE

HAS PERSONAL DEVELOPMENT sparked something inside of you? Do the moments we have shared in our book inspire you? If so, THERE IS MORE! We have completed a companion guide to compliment the lessons shared in this book, you can put these moments into practice in your own life to see doggone amazing results.

We have only scratched the surface of each topic. There is so much more for us to explore. In the companion guide you will be given the opportunity to reflect, answer, as well as get practical step-by-step guidance to improving your life. Knowledge is powerful, but if we do not implement it by putting it into practice then it becomes just another dusty book on the shelf…just another cute story we read. The companion guide is created to help you take action! You will get to dig deeper into topics like:

- 🐾 How to make forgiveness easy and painless.

- 🐾 How to listen better and "hear" what people are *really* saying.

- 🐾 The top 3 tricks that will help you stay grounded through any storm.

❧ How you can actually use your past to propel you into your future.

❧ How *Adversity* can be your *Advantage*.

One of the philosophies I live by is this: With all of the opportunities in front of each of us to invest our time and money, investing in our own personal development will yield a far greater return than any other venture. You *are* your most valuable asset. Miley and I believe that you are worth investing in, so come and join us in the companion guide and lets get started. You will truly learn to "Put Your Best Paw Forward."

Tara & Miley,

P.S. You are not alone, Miley and I will be with you the whole walk!